DATE DUE   JAN   2014

	WITHDRAWN		

GHOSTS
AND OTHER SPIRITS OF THE DEAD

by Ruth Owen

Consultant: Troy Taylor
President of the American Ghost Society

BEARPORT
PUBLISHING

New York, New York

Credits

Cover and Title Page, ©Andreas Gradin/Shutterstock and ©Christina Richards/Shutterstock; 4–5, ©Kim Jones; 6, ©Bettmann/Corbis; 7, ©FloridaStock/Shutterstock and Wikipedia Creative Commons; 8–9, ©Andy Clarke/Shutterstock, ©Kiselev Andrey Valerevich/Shutterstock, and ©Paul Hakimata Photography/Shutterstock; 10–11, ©LianeM/Shutterstock, ©Jaimie Duplass/Shutterstock, and ©Kiselev Andrey Valerevich/Shutterstock; 12–13, ©Leszek Gadula/Alamy; 13T, ©PHCS W.M. Cox, U.S. Navy; 13B, ©Stuart Monk/Shutterstock and ©David Ewing Photography/Shutterstock; 14–15, ©Olly/Shutterstock, ©Quetton/Shutterstock, and ©Plastique/Shutterstock; 16–17, ©Kim Jones; 18, ©Mikael Buck/Rex Features; 19, ©Graham Morris/Topfoto; 20–21, ©Zorik Galstyan/Shutterstock; 21T, ©Jupiter Images/Getty Images/Thinkstock; 21B, ©J Paget RF photos/Shutterstock; 22, ©Nutech21/Shutterstock; 23, ©Renee Keith/Getty Images; 24, ©Peter D./Shutterstock; 25, ©Dale O'Dell/Alamy; 26–27, ©Grischa Georgiew/Shutterstock and ©Jeff Thrower/Shutterstock; 28L, ©Annette Shaff/Shutterstock; 28R, ©Losevsky Photo and Video/Shutterstock and ©Everett Collection/Shutterstock; 29L, ©Sir Simon Marsden/The Marsden Archive/Alamy; 29R, ©Andrew L./Shutterstock.

Publisher: Kenn Goin
Senior Editor: Joyce Tavolacci
Creative Director: Spencer Brinker
Design: Emma Randall
Editor: Mark J. Sachner
Photo Researcher: Ruby Tuesday Books Ltd

Library of Congress Cataloging-in-Publication Data in process at time of publication (2013)
Library of Congress Control Number: 2012039959
ISBN-13: 978-1-61772-724-5 (library binding)

For more information, write to Bearport Publishing Company, Inc., 45 West 21st Street, Suite 3B, New York, New York 10010. Printed in the United States of America.

10 9 8 7 6 5 4 3 2 1

Contents

A Disappearing Passenger

It was an ordinary day at New Jersey's Newark Airport in 1973. A flight crew was preparing an Eastern Air Lines jumbo jet for takeoff. After counting the passengers, flight attendant Sis Patterson found she had one too many. The extra passenger was a man dressed in an Eastern Air Lines captain's uniform. Sis approached the man and asked him several times who he was. The man did not respond. Instead, he stared straight ahead, seemingly unaware of her presence.

Eventually, the flight's captain left the **cockpit** to question the silent passenger. The captain took one look at the strange man and gasped, "My God, it's Bob Loft!" Suddenly, the man vanished. Sis and the captain were stunned. The disappearing passenger was Captain Robert Loft, an Eastern Air Lines pilot who had been killed in the horrible crash of Flight 401, just a few months before!

One Passenger Too Many

Before takeoff, flight attendants match the number of people aboard a plane with the number of passengers on a list. At first, Sis Patterson thought the extra passenger was a pilot getting a last-minute ride to another airport for his next job.

The Victims of Flight 401

On December 29, 1972, Captain Loft was flying Eastern Air Lines Flight 401 from New York to Miami. As the plane approached Miami, however, something went disastrously wrong. The plane began to lose **altitude**. When Captain Loft and flight engineer Don Repo finally discovered that the plane was only a few hundred feet above the ground, it was too late.

Just before midnight, Flight 401 crashed into the dark swamps of the Florida Everglades. The terrible accident killed 101 people.

After the crash, two of the victims, Captain Loft and Don Repo, began to haunt Eastern Air Lines planes. For nearly 18 months, the ghostly flight crew appeared on planes. Then the sightings died out, and the two ghosts of Flight 401 have never been seen again.

Captain Robert Loft

Flight Engineer Don Repo

This picture shows what experts believe were the final moments of Flight 401.

A Ghostly Warning

One day, Don Repo's face appeared inside an aircraft. Repo warned the plane's engineer: "Watch out for fire on this airplane." A few days later, one of the plane's engines caught fire, but thankfully

What Are Ghosts?

People have reported seeing ghosts for thousands of years. What are these strange and sometimes terrifying **apparitions**? The most common belief is that ghosts are the **spirits** of people or animals who have died. Many people believe that a spirit is the life force, or energy, inside a living thing. When a person or animal dies, the spirit is said to sometimes remain behind with the living.

According to believers, a ghost might be the spirit of a person who died in a tragic way. For example, the person may have been murdered or killed in a car accident. Because the ghost is unable to find peace after death, it haunts the place where the tragedy occurred.

Good and Bad Ghosts

Many people believe that some ghosts want to harm the living. Other ghosts, like flight engineer Don Repo, seem to want to help people.

Different Ghost Forms

What was that tall, dark shape at the end of the hallway? Who was the deathly pale little girl peeking from behind a headstone in the graveyard? Ghosts, it seems, can **materialize** in many different forms.

Some witnesses who have seen ghosts say they appear as solid, lifelike figures—just like the ghostly pilot of Flight 401. The spirits may appear at night, in the middle of the day, or in a crowded place. The witnesses believe they are looking at living people—until the ghosts disappear before their very eyes!

Other ghosts are said to be see-through, or transparent. Still others appear as wispy, mysterious shapes that vanish in a matter of seconds.

Ghostly visitors don't always show themselves to people, however. Witnesses may simply hear moaning, singing, screaming, or crying.

Smelly Ghosts

Sometimes, people notice a smell that suddenly appears out of nowhere and then disappears again. Ghostly smells may include perfume or the smell of something burning.

The USS *Hornet*

More than 300 sailors suffered sudden and violent deaths aboard the U.S. Navy aircraft carrier, the USS *Hornet*. As a result, many people report seeing the ghosts of the sailors who were tragically killed.

The USS *Hornet* was in service from 1943 to 1970. During its 27 years at sea, the ship fought in **World War II** (1939–1945) and other conflicts. Some of the ship's crew were killed in wartime battles. Others, however, died in horrific accidents aboard the ship. For example, some sailors were killed when the thick wire used to **catapult** aircraft off the deck of the ship suddenly snapped. As the wire sprung back, it sliced through any person in its path. Since then, a headless ghost has been seen onboard the ship. Some people believe it's the spirit of a sailor **decapitated** by the wire.

Who's There?

Sailors aboard the USS *Hornet* have heard doors open and close and toilets flush when no one is around. Some people report being grabbed or pushed by something when they are completely alone.

The USS *Hornet* in service

Ghostly Road

It's not just planes, ships, and graveyards where restless, **tormented** spirits appear. In the case of Bloods Point Road in Boone County, Illinois, a whole road has become the setting for nightly **supernatural** activity!

By day, Bloods Point Road is a typical road. At night, however, drivers report seeing terrifying things that cannot be explained. Cars are sometimes followed by a large, black truck that appears and disappears. At other times, old school buses, pickup trucks, and even a police car appear out of nowhere and then vanish.

According to one story, many children were once killed on the road when their school bus crashed on a bridge. Travelers on Bloods Point Road sometimes hear the children's screams or see small, ghostly figures alongside the road.

Ghostly Handprints

Some drivers say they have found unexplained, child-sized handprints on their cars after they've driven along Bloods Point Road.

Poltergeists

Some ghosts appear and disappear quietly. Others make contact with the living, speaking to people and passing on warnings of future danger. There is one type of ghost, however, that is noisy, destructive, and even violent.

If a chair has just flown through the air, or a vase falls from a shelf for no reason, there could be a **poltergeist** in the room. Poltergeists are noisy ghosts that smash things and move furniture around—even large, heavy objects, such as dressers and tables. Some victims of poltergeists have been pinched or hit by the ghosts. Others have been lifted into the air and slammed against walls!

What makes a ghost attack the living? No one knows for sure. One explanation could be that the angry ghost does not want to share its home with someone new.

A Noisy Spirit

The word *poltergeist* comes from the German word, *poltern*, which means "to make noise or knock," and the word *geist*, which means "a spirit, or ghost."

The Enfield Poltergeist

Janet Hodgson was just 11 years old when a poltergeist began haunting her family's home at 284 Green Street in Enfield, England. The frightening events began the night of August 30, 1977, when Janet's bed started violently shaking. In the weeks that followed, there were strange knocking noises in the walls of Janet's house. Heavy pieces of furniture mysteriously moved across rooms.

Sometimes Janet herself was picked up by some unseen force and thrown across the room. Police officers, newspaper reporters, and **paranormal investigators** came to the house. They, too, witnessed these strange events.

After about a year, the strange happenings gradually died down. Today, Janet still believes in the poltergeist that terrorized her and her family.

284 Green Street, Enfield, England

An unseen force throws Janet Hodgson across her bedroom. Janet's sister, Rose, screams in terror.

The Voice of Bill Wilkins

The poltergeist that haunted Janet and her family was believed to be Bill Wilkins, an old man who had died at 284 Green Street many years before. Sometimes, Bill spoke through Janet in the growling, eerie voice of an elderly man.

Deathly Dog

The ghosts of animals are also believed to roam the earth. At Hanging Hills, in Meriden, Connecticut, a small black dog is said to haunt the rocky cliffs. **Legends** dating back to the 1800s say that if a person sees the dog three times, he or she will die.

According to one story, in 1898, a **geologist** named W.H.C. Pyncheon came across a small, black dog while studying the rocks at Hanging Hills. Three years later, Pyncheon and another scientist, Herbert Marshall, were rock climbing together, not far from where Pyncheon first saw the dog. Marshall joked that he had seen the black dog twice before. As the men climbed, the black dog suddenly appeared on a rocky ledge nearby. Within moments, Marshall slipped and fell to his death!

Six years later, Pyncheon went climbing again at Hanging Hills. This time, he was alone. Not long after, his body was found beneath the cliffs. Did Pyncheon meet the little black dog a third time, too?

The Silent Bark

The black dog of Hanging Hills is said to look like a spaniel. The ghostly dog leaves no paw prints in the mud or snow, and when it opens its mouth to bark, no sounds come out.

21

Contacting the Dead

Some people encounter ghosts unwillingly. Others, however, want to make contact with spirits of the dead by holding a **séance**.

In a darkened room, a small group of people gather around a table. The séance is led by a **medium**—a person with the power to communicate with the dead. The medium often goes into a **trance**. Then he or she hears messages from spirits, and passes the messages on to people in the room. Usually, the messages are from the people's dead relatives or friends.

Many people believe that séances are simply a trick and that the messages are made up. Many others, however, believe that mediums really can talk to spirits and relay important messages from beyond the grave.

Ghostly Spelling

Some people use Ouija boards to communicate with spirits. Each person using the board puts a finger on a small piece of wood called a planchette. If a spirit has a message for one of the people, it moves the planchette around the board to different letters to spell out words.

YES

NO

Ouija board

ABCDEFGHIJKLM
NOPQRSTUVWXYZ
4567890
OOD BYE

planchette

23

Fact or Fiction?

If ghosts aren't the spirits of the dead, what are they? One explanation is that ghostly visions are examples of people's minds playing tricks on them.

For instance, people who are very tired or sick with a fever can experience **hallucinations** or confuse real life with dreams. They might see ghostly figures that don't really exist or hear spooky sounds, such as a person wailing, in a room that is perfectly silent.

Sometimes, a person will catch a glimpse of something that's hard to make out. The person cannot process what's been seen quickly enough, so the brain fills in the gaps in vision with a picture of a human shape from the person's memory. When the person takes a closer look, however, he or she realizes that the ghostly vision was just a shadow.

Is it a ghost? Or is the dark figure just a shadow in a spooky hallway?

Does this old photo show a ghostly woman, or is it a computer trick?

A close-up view of the ghostly figure's face

Portrait of a Ghost?

Some people claim to have taken photos of ghosts. However, many of these photos turn out to be fakes. People can **superimpose** a ghostly image onto any background image using special computer programs. Anyone with a computer and a good imagination can create a portrait of a ghost.

Ghost Hunters

Ghost hunters are like detectives who investigate ghostly **phenomena**. A ghost hunter carefully examines a building where eerie things are said to be taking place. He or she may also research the building's history to find out if someone was murdered or if another tragic event took place there.

In addition, ghost hunters interview people who have witnessed strange happenings. They may also set up a **vigil** in a haunted place to keep watch for any ghosts. Often, ghost hunters find an explanation for weird phenomena. For example, noises in an attic may just be a family of mice.

Sometimes, however, the only explanation seems to be that something supernatural, or as yet unexplained, is sharing a person's home. Could it be the spirit of a dead person? Is it possible that ghosts exist and roam the world alongside the living? No one knows for sure. The search for answers goes on. . . .

Ghost-Hunting Equipment

- A notebook and pen
- A camera
- A video camera
- A motion detector, for picking up small movements
- A watch, for accurately timing events
- The most important tool is an open mind—don't jump to conclusions! Instead, collect and examine the evidence.

Ghosts Around the World

Here are profiles of famous ghosts that witnesses claim to have seen, heard, and even photographed. Check out who's who in the world of ghosts and the ghostly deeds of these restless spirits.

The Phantom Hitchhiker of Bluebell Hill

Location: Bluebell Hill, Kent, England

Description: The ghost is a young woman believed to be one of three friends killed in a terrible car crash on Bluebell Hill on the night of November 19, 1965.

Ghostly deeds: The ghost hitchhikes to the nearby town of Maidstone—the place where the young woman was heading on the night of her death. When a car stops to pick her up, she gets into the back seat but then vanishes.

The Toys "R" Us Ghost

Location: Toys "R" Us, Sunnyvale, California

Description: The Toys "R" Us ghost is said to be a farm worker named Johnny Johnson. In the 1800s, Johnny lived and worked on a ranch that stood where the toy store stands today. While chopping wood with an axe one day, Johnny accidentally hacked into his leg and bled to death.

Ghostly deeds: Johnny makes dolls and trucks jump off the store's shelves. Sometimes, he causes balls to bounce along the aisles.

The Brown Lady

Location: Raynham Hall, Norfolk, England

Description: The Brown Lady is a ghostly woman wearing a long, brown dress. Her eyes are black, empty sockets. The ghost is believed to be Lady Dorothy Townshend, who was locked away in Raynham Hall by her cruel husband. She died a prisoner in the house in the 1700s.

Ghostly deeds: The Brown Lady walks the corridors of Raynham Hall and appears on the large staircase. In 1936, she appeared before two photographers, and her ghostly shape was captured in the photograph above.

D.C. (the Demon Cat of the Capitol)

Location: The U.S. Capitol basement, Washington, DC

Description: When a person first spots D.C., it looks like a small black kitten. As D.C. approaches the person, however, the cat grows to the size of a tiger.

Ghostly deeds: D.C. was originally put into the basement to catch rats. Now it prowls the capitol's basement terrorizing security guards. When spotted, the cat pounces at a person, but vanishes in mid-air before attacking.

29

Glossary

altitude (AL-ti-*tood*) the height above sea level

apparitions (*ap*-uh-RISH-uhnz) ghosts or ghostlike images

catapult (KAT-uh-*puhlt*) to hurl or launch something

cockpit (KOK-pit) the area in the front of a plane where the pilot sits

decapitated (dee-KAP-uh-*tay*-tid) to have had one's head cut off

geologist (jee-OL-uh-jist) a scientist who studies rocks and soil

hallucinations (huh-*loo*-suh-NAY-shuhnz) things that are seen or heard that aren't really there

legends (LEJ-uhndz) stories handed down from long ago that are often based on some facts but cannot be proven true

materialize (muh-TEER-ee-uh-lize) to take on a form or come into being

medium (MEE-dee-uhm) a person through whom others seek to communicate with the dead

paranormal investigators (*pa*-ruh-NOR-muhl in-VEST-uh-*gay*-torz) people who study events or collect information about things that cannot be scientifically explained

phenomena (fuh-NOM-uh-nuh) occurrences that one can see or feel

poltergeist (POHL-tur-gyest) a disruptive ghost that makes loud noises and moves objects

séance (SAY-ahnss) a gathering at which people try to communicate with the dead

spirits (SPIHR-its) supernatural creatures, such as ghosts

superimpose (*soo*-pur-im-POSE) to place one thing over another, so both are visible

supernatural (*soo*-pur-NACH-ur-uhl) having to do with something that breaks the laws of nature

tormented (tor-MEN-tid) experiencing severe physical or mental suffering

trance (TRANSS) a half-conscious or hypnotic state

vigil (VIJ-uhl) keeping watch, usually for a long time

World War II (WURLD WOR TOO) a worldwide conflict from 1939 to 1945 that involved many countries

Bibliography

American Hauntings: www.prairieghosts.com

Association for the Scientific Study of Anomalous Phenomena: www.assap.ac.uk/newsite/articles/Ghosts.html

Fuller, John G. *The Ghost of Flight 401.* London: Souvenir Press (1976).

Read More

Krensky, Stephen. *Ghosts (Monster Chronicles).* Minneapolis, MN: Lerner (2008).

Pipe, Jim. *Ghosts (Tales of Horror).* New York: Bearport (2007).

Walker, Kathryn, and Brian Innes. *The Mystery of the Ghosts of Flight 401 (Unsolved!).* New York: Crabtree (2009).

Learn More Online

To learn more about ghosts, visit
www.bearportpublishing.com/NotNearNormal

Index

About the Author

Ruth Owen has been developing, editing, and writing children's books for more than ten years. She lives in Cornwall, England, just minutes from the ocean. Ruth loves gardening and caring for her family of llamas.